I Am Fruitful

Walking in the Fruit of the Spirit

Book Six

Walking with Jesus

Becoming the Best Me I Can Be

Pamela D White

All scripture quotations, unless otherwise indicated, are taken from the Holy Bible, **New King James Version©**. Copyright © 1982 by Thomas Nelson, Inc. Used by permission. All rights reserved.

Scripture quotations marked NIV are taken from the Holy Bible, **New International Version**®, NIV®. Copyright © 1973, 1978, 1984 by **Biblica, Inc.**® **Used by permission. All rights reserved worldwide.**

Scripture quotations marked NASB are taken from the Holy Bible, **New American Standard Bible**®, Copyright © 1960, 1971, 1977, 1995, 2020 by The Lockman Foundation. All rights reserved.

Scripture quotations marked AMP are taken from the Holy Bible, **Amplified**, copyright © 2015 by The Lockman Foundation, La Habra, CA 90631. All rights reserved. For Permission To Quote information visit http://www.lockman.org/

Scripture quotations marked ESV are taken from the ESV® Bible (The Holy Bible, **English Standard Version**®). ESV® Text Edition: 2016. Copyright © 2001 by Crossway, a publishing ministry of Good News Publishers. The ESV® text has been reproduced in cooperation with and by permission of Good News Publishers. Unauthorized reproduction of this publication is prohibited. All rights reserved.

Scripture quotations marked NLT are taken from the Holy Bible, **New Living Translation,** copyright © 1996, 2004, 2015 by Tyndale House Foundation. Used by permission of Tyndale House Publishers, Inc., Carol Stream, Illinois 60188. All rights reserved.

Scripture quotations marked MSG are taken from **THE MESSAGE**, copyright © 1993, 2002, 2018 by Eugene H. Peterson. Used by permission of NavPress. All rights reserved. Represented by Tyndale House Publishers, Inc.

Scripture quotations marked AKJV are taken from the Holy Bible, **Authorized King James Version**, The Authorized (King James) Version of the Bible ('the KJV'), the rights in which are vested in the Crown in the United Kingdom, is reproduced here by permission of the Crown's patentee, Cambridge University Press. The Cambridge KJV text, including paragraphing, is reproduced here by permission of Cambridge University Press.

Scripture quotations marked KJV are taken from the Holy Bible, **King James Version**.

A publication of Blooming Desert Ministries

ISBN 978-1-7370803-0-5 (sc print)
ISBN 978-1-7370803-1-2 (ebook)

Printed in the United States of America
Copyright © 2021 by Pamela D White
All Rights Reserved.

IngramSparks Publishing (Ingram: Lightning Source, LLC)

One Ingram Blvd., La Vergne, TN 37086

Publishing Note: Publishing style capitalizes certain pronouns in Scriptures that refer to the Father, Son, and Holy Spirit, and may differ from other publishing styles. **All emphasis in the Scriptures' quotations is the authors.** The name satan and related names are not capitalized as the author's preference not to acknowledge him, even though it violates grammatical rules.

No part of this book may be reproduced or transmitted in any form or by any means, electronic or mechanical – including photocopying, recording, or by any information storage and retrieval system – without permission in writing from the publisher. Please direct inquires to PDW Publications.

PDW PUBLICATIONS

Dedication

This book series is dedicated to you.

Everyone has opportunities to become a better version of themselves. My prayer is that this book series helps you on that journey. The Lord loves you so much He desires an intimate relationship with you. You are special to Him and He loves spending time with you. Walking and talking with Jesus every day should be the norm, not the exception. Life can bring difficult circumstances and situations. When you walk with Jesus, life events, are not only manageable but can be turned for your good.

"And we know that all things work together for good to those who love God, to those who are the called according to His purpose," Romans 8:28.

Come with me into this exploration of how you can develop a relationship with Jesus and walk with Him every day. This is an opportunity to become a better you.

Acknowledgments

The Great Commission given by our Lord and Savior Jesus Christ noted in Matthew 28:16-20 is my inspiration for this publication. Verses 19-20 state, *"Go therefore and make disciples of all the nations, baptizing them in the name of the Father and of the Son and of the Holy Spirit, teaching them to observe all things that I have commanded you; and lo, I am with you always, even to the end of the age."* This verse is the very basis for missionary work all over the globe. I have been blessed to be able to serve in a few of those missions. Missions are an amazing experience. I came to realize though that everyone cannot always do all the parts commanded in these verses. I can't always go. I didn't often get to baptize. What I realized was that I can do my part in teaching to observes the truths of the Scriptures. My desire to fulfill the teaching part of the Great Commission was the inspiration for this work. My pastor, Bishop Larry Taylor, and First Lady Desetra Taylor allowed our church to use these Bible studies in our New Life Discipleship classes for nearly twenty years. The work has also been used in prison ministries in central Illinois for as many years. The teaching has proven effective in changing many lives and discipling the children of God. Thank you, Bishop and First Lady, for teaching a balanced spiritual and natural life so I could complete this project and see the impact of the work on people's lives.

Bishop positioned me to be the director of New Life Ministries Discipleship for several years. New Life classes were designed to teach those new to Christianity or new to the church the foundational truths needed to build a solid life in Christ. During that time, this work was fine-tuned with the help and input from the dedicated, gifted, and anointed New Life teachers Minister Retta Smith, Minister James Smith, Minister Debby Henkel, Dr. Terry Husband, Minister Char-Michelle McDowell, Minister Yvonne Smith, Minister Herbert Smyer, and Professor Susan Gibson along with the encouragement and guidance of Dr. Chequita Brown and community service advocate Minister Patricia Turner. I also want to give a shout-out to Dr. Wanda Turner, nationally acclaimed minister, teacher, prophet, life coach, mentor, and best-selling author, who continued to encourage me to just publish the thing! Thanks to all of you. Each of you has made a significant impact on my life.

My dear friend and mentor, First Lady Marshell Wickware, supported the project and pushed me to publish it for years. Thanks for not giving up on me!

My life-long friend, Robin McClallen, thank you for all your support, input, and encouraging me to publish something. You have been instrumental in making me an author.

A special thanks to my husband, Brian K. White, for his patience and prayers as I spent hours and hours researching, writing, and rewriting. Thanks, BW!

Most of all thank you to the Holy Spirit and my Lord and Savior Jesus Christ. I present this work in obedience and honor to You.

Contents

Introduction	11
Definition of Fruit of the Spirit	13
Become a Fruit Bearer	17
Fruit of the Spirit—Galatians 5:22-23	19
Love	19
Joy	21
Peace	23
Long-suffering	24
Kindness	27
Goodness	28
Faithfulness	29
Gentleness	31
Temperance	33
Hindrances	35
Stepping Stones	47
I Am Fruitful	49
Mountain vs. Valley	43
Glossary	51
About the Author	57

Book Six

I Am Fruitful
Walking in the Fruit of the Spirit

OBJECTIVE

Fruit of the Spirit is a biblical term describing nine attributes of Christ that become evident in the life of a person who submitted their life to the Lord. In your humanity, you may exhibit a replica or model of some spiritual fruit. However, without the Holy Spirit functioning in your life, your fruit will be tainted. This lesson discusses the true Fruit of the Spirit.

MEMORY VERSE

"But the fruit of the Spirit is love, joy, peace, forbearance, kindness, goodness, faithfulness, gentleness and self-control. Against such things there is no law," Galatians 5:22-23.

I Am Fruitful

A. Definition of the Fruit of the Spirit

B. Becoming a Fruit-Bearer
1. Love
2. Joy
3. Peace
4. Long-suffering
5. Kindness
6. Goodness
7. Faithfulness
8. Gentleness
9. Temperance (Self-Control)

C. Hindrances
1. Fear
2. High-mindedness
3. Ignorance
4. Comparisons
5. Neglect
6. Criticism
7. Worry
8. Sin
9. Complacency

D. Mountain vs Valley

Book Six

I Am Fruitful

Walking in the Fruit of the Spirit

Introduction

The Fruits of the Spirit are character traits that develop in God's children. The Fruits of the Spirit are not gifts like the spiritual gifts we discussed in Book Four – *I Am Supernatural*. Spiritual gifts are special, supernatural gifts given through the Holy Spirit used to encourage others. Fruits of the Spirit are attributes of the Holy Spirit evident in God's people, not gifts. The Greek word used for fruit in this passage is *karpos* which means results, profit, or gain. Fruit results from being filled with the Spirit of God. You are not only a creation of God, but you carry God with you wherever you go. You are made in His image and have been given the Holy Spirit to live in you as a guide and comfort. God has made you His representative to the world. Therefore, part of your transformation from sin to righteousness is developing the characteristics of God. Those characteristics are called fruit.

Definition of Fruit of the Spirit

First, let's talk about what fruit is. When thinking about fruit, an apple might come to mind. Perhaps you might think of an orange, banana, or mango. Fruit is sweet and fleshy and contains seeds. Botanically, fruit is a seed-bearing structure that developed from the ovary of a flowering plant. Fruit is usually edible and often sweet. It is also nutritious and needed to sustain a healthy life. Fruit is a product of fertilization and contains the means for reproduction. You can save your apple seeds and plant them to **REPRODUCE** multiple apple trees for multiplied apple production, just like Johnny Appleseed did all those years ago.

The Bible often describes spiritual things in terms that are easily understood, especially at the time the authors wrote it. Jesus often described spiritual teaching in agricultural terms. Most people understand fruit and you can learn about spiritual fruit by looking at natural fruit. How does the Fruit of the Spirit compare to natural fruit? As noted, fruit is a product of fertilization. Two things came together to produce the fruit, the ovary, and the pollen. Spiritual fruit also is a product of two things coming together, you and the Holy Spirit. Spiritual fruit cannot grow and develop without the Holy Spirit involved. When the ovary of a flower is pollinated the fruit develops. When the Holy Spirit fills your heart, spiritual fruit develops. You know fruit comes in all shapes and sizes, and one of the major functions of fruit is seed dispersal to encourage the growth of additional plants. One of your primary functions as a child of God in union with the Holy Spirit is to reproduce. The Lord commands reproduction frequently. Genesis 9:1 says, *"And as for you, be fruitful and multiply; bring forth abundantly in the earth and multiply in it."*

You are to encourage the growth of more children of God. Fruit is pretty tasty when ready for picking. Nobody wants sour, moldy fruit. Rotten fruit isn't nutritious either. Same with people. They don't want some Christian with a sour attitude and moldy ideas to tell them what to do. You win people to Christ through love and nurturing. Good fruit is highly nutritious and life-sustaining, as is the Fruit of the Spirit.

Essentially, **YOU ARE LIKE A TREE**, rooted and grounded in Christ, producing fruit for others: your family, your friends, your neighbors, your coworkers, and maybe even nations.

"How blessed is the man who does not walk in the counsel of the wicked, nor stand in the path of sinners, nor sit in the seat of scoffers! But his delight is in the law of the LORD, and in His law he meditates day and night. He will be like a tree firmly planted by streams of water, which yields its fruit in its season and its leaf does not wither; and in whatever he does, he prospers," Psalm 1:1-3 NASB.

Now you know you are like a tree with fruit, but what is the fruit? Fruit are the nine specific character traits that develop in you and work through you as you grow and develop because of the Holy Spirit working in your life. Do you remember the talking trees on the Wizard of Oz that threw apples at Dorothy and the Scarecrow? They were not willing to share their fruit, then got nasty with the fruit they have. Hoarding your fruit is never what God intended. The fruit in your life is there for you to **SHARE** with others. The way you react to situations and others should come from your fruit. Your decisions should filter through your fruit. How you treat others should be full of fruit. What are these characteristics called the Fruit of the Spirit? These attributes are love, joy, peace, longsuffering, gentleness, goodness, faith, meekness, and temperance. The Fruits of the Spirit are found in Galatians 5:22-23 and are the visible attributes that show a productive Christian life.

Become a Fruit Bearer

When you commit your life to follow Christ, having Christ dwell in your hearts by faith, you become a new creature. Your old nature is no longer in control; nor are you a slave to the bondage of sin. Christ has made you free. Through your spiritual connection with the Holy Spirit, you can now produce fruitful behavior that is rooted in holiness.

The Fruit of the Spirit is the manifestation of God's love through you by the power of the Holy Spirit. It is the OUTWARD EVIDENCE of your inward relationship with Christ. Though there are nine attributes listed, the word *fruit* is singular, meaning they work as one. You cannot pick which attribute to desire or develop; it's all or nothing!

"But the fruit of the Spirit is love, joy, peace, longsuffering, gentleness, goodness, faith, meekness, temperance: against such there is no law," Galatians 5:22-23 KJV.

Fruit of the Spirit—Galatians 5:22-23

Love	Joy	Peace
Patience (long-suffering)	Gentleness	Goodness
Faith	Meekness	Temperance (self-control)

Love

Years ago, I heard a Bible teacher discussing the Fruit of the Spirit, and they used the illustration of a shower curtain and shower rod. Love represented the shower rod. The other eight fruit all hung from the rod. Without love, none of the rest of the fruit will function. The Bible doesn't differentiate that one fruit is more important than the other, but the concept is valid. 1 John 4:8 tells us that God is love. Without God, you can't show godly love or develop spiritual fruit.

In order not to misinterpret your emotions concerning love, it is important to understand the different forms of love found in scripture references or examples.

There are two forms of love discussed in the scriptures: unconditional and conditional. Conditional love is represented by the Greek words, Phileo and Eros. Phileo love is a platonic love that is warm, tender, and affectionate. You feel this type of love in your human emotions. Phileo love describes the love of friends and family. It is a chosen love. Therefore, it places restrictions, conditions, or provisions on that love. This type of love usually contains 'if' (example: if you don't betray me I will love you, if you act like I think you should, if you say the right things, if you give me a gift on my birthday—then I'll love you).

Eros love is erotic, physical love experienced with passion and romantic feelings. This love may be strong at the beginning of a relationship. A relationship based on eros love will quickly fail, as there is no substance to eros love. Eros can be dangerous, as there is often a loss of control associated with eros love.

The Bible also talks about storge love, which is family love. This is the love a parent feels for a child or the love a family member feels for another family member. Storge love may have some unconditional qualities such as a mother's love for a flawed child, however, it does not have the power of agape love as storge love may have limitations and still operates out of your humanity.

Unconditional love in Greek is the word agape. Agape has no conditions or 'ifs' to function. Agape love sees beyond the outer surface and accepts the other person regardless of their flaws, faults, or behaviors because it's spiritual love. The word agape is a verb requiring action or behavior that shows unconditional love. Though one may not like someone, you can choose to love them as a creation of God. **AGAPE LOVE IS SACRIFICIAL**, as you expect nothing in return for the acceptance that has been offered. Agape love is not possessive or demanding and can only be found through the Holy Spirit. This is the love that is the shower rod all the other fruit hang from. It is impossible to show unconditional agape love to others in your natural humanity. You must have the Holy Spirit living in and through you to show agape love. Those who show agape love exhibit the nature of God, which is all based on the Lord's most dominant character trait and the essence of who God is - love.

"And we know and have believed the love which God hath in us. God is love; and he that abideth in love abideth in God, and God abideth in him," 1 John 4:16 KJV.

Love is something that will never cease. Other things may pass away or cease to be needed but love is forever.

1 Corinthians 13:4-8 is the best description of love.

"Love is patient, love is kind. It does not envy, it does not boast, it is not proud. It does not dishonor others, it is not self-seeking, it is not easily angered, it keeps no record of wrongs. Love does not delight in evil but rejoices with the truth. It always protects, always trusts, always hopes, always perseveres. Love never fails. But where there are prophecies, they will cease; where there are tongues, they will be stilled; where there is knowledge, it will pass away," NIV.

JOY

Before we talk about what joy is, let's talk about what joy isn't. Joy is not happiness. People often base happiness on material things, events, or emotions. Someone gives you a present for your birthday or Christmas and it makes you happy until it breaks or the new wears off. You get a new car and you are happy until you have to make payments. Happiness is a natural emotion or a reaction based on an emotional response. Nowhere in the Bible are you promised consistent happiness. Joy, however, is promised. **JOY CAN BE YOURS EVERY DAY.** It is more than a temporary good feeling. Joy is a spiritual emotion, not a natural emotion. It does not mean you feel good all the time. Joy is an assurance that can't be shaken. Deep down in your soul, you know without a shadow of doubt that despite how bleak things might look, everything will be all right because God is in control. Joy allows you to praise God all the time no matter what is happening, good or bad.

You can have joy despite your deepest sorrows and while racked in pain. Joy is yours even when your car is repossessed. You can have joy while you watch a loved one cross to the other side of life. Joy strengthens you while you watch the doctor put a cast on your child's arm. That doesn't mean you are glad those things happened. It means that despite the situation; you know that you know that you know that everything will be all right and God is still in your corner. He is watching over you and has never left you. Joy is not relative to the situation. It is your strength despite situations. Joy gives strength because when you know your God is an almighty God that is more powerful than any situation, you can overcome anything.

When others see the joy of the Lord operating through you regardless of your situation, it draws them to the Lord. This is how joy reproduces. The stability joy brings makes others question how you do it! You will be asked, "How do you stay so strong?" This opens the door wide to tell them about the joy of the Lord and plant the seed of joy.

"Then he said to them, Go your way, eat the fat, and drink the sweet, and send portions to them for whom nothing is prepared: for this day is holy to our Lord: neither be you sorry; for the joy of the Lord is your strength," Nehemiah 8:10 AKJV.

Peace

The Greek word used for peace in Galatians 5 is the word *eirene*. It has a very full meaning, but a very important thing to glean from the word peace is that it means 'rest.' Rest has an enormous meaning in the Bible. To have rest is to no longer struggle with sin and bondage. You are free from that turmoil through salvation, so you have rest which brings peace. You no longer need to be concerned with your eternal destination when you believe Jesus. You have the assurance you will live forever with Him. This gives your soul rest and peace. Your relationship with the Lord will bring you freedom from things that kept you in bondage. You are no longer bound to the things of this world but are now bound to a heavenly destiny, so you **REST** and have peace. Though the world rages around you in various situations, peace means you have it all together despite the mess you see.

You cannot attain peace through any physical or emotional means. Human nature is to be selfish and leads to contentions and jealousies and a variety of other unpeaceful emotions that bring unrest. When you invite the Holy Spirit into your life, He works a harmony and calm that only manifest through the Holy Spirit. Peace operates because you trust God in situations. Peace is not just about your spiritual relationship with God. He is a total God and a God of balance. Peace also refers to peace in your body, which is freedom from sickness and disease. Peace means you have health and well-being, safety and harmony. It also means you are not a slave to debt and poverty but can **REST** in the prosperity of God, free from the worries and financial turmoil of the world. Peace is the inner tranquility and contentment of the believer whose trust is in God.

Matthew 5:9 says, *"Blessed are the peacemakers, for they will be called sons of God."* Some get confused about the difference between a peacekeeper and a peacemaker. A peacekeeper seeks to keep peace by avoiding conflict. They give in to tension and avoid disagreements. This is not the way of the Lord. A peacemaker is someone who will resolve both the inner and outer turmoil of others. This is the way of the Lord and how you reproduce peace. When a person lives a sinful life without the Lord, they have no peace. As you walk in peace, become a peacemaker, and lead others to peace, you will plant seeds of peace in others.

Romans 15:13 "Now the God of hope fill you with all joy and peace in believing, that you may abound in hope, through the power of the Holy Ghost," AKJV.

LONG-SUFFERING

The Greek word *makrothymia* is translated as long-suffering. Long-suffering is the act of enduring or suffering in the face of adversity. It can be interpreted as long-tempered or holding your temper for a long time. It is also translated as **PATIENCE**, endurance, steadfastness, perseverance, and forbearance. A patient person can endure much suffering and pain without complaining. People can endure a lot of things. Can you endure without complaining? Human nature complains about circumstances. Patience endures. A patient person is also slow to anger. Proverbs 16:36

says, *"Whoever is slow to anger is better than the mighty, and he who rules his spirit than he who takes a city."* This type of patience is not so much focused on circumstances as it is on people.

God extended long-suffering or patience towards you despite your sinful ways. He patiently waited on you to give up sin believed in Jesus Christ. He gently guided you toward the truth. It was His patience that led you to repentance. In like manner, you are expected to exercise longsuffering (patience) toward others. Patience is a position of power. You may be in a position to take revenge on someone when you feel wronged. With the patience of the Holy Spirit, you have a supernatural ability to exercise self-restraint and let God be your defender. People can push your buttons and make you feel frustrated, confused, angry, and can make you want to give up on them, letting them choose their way through life. Patience will keep you in check and strong. Letting go of self-restraint shows a weakness. Those who let go of self-restraint might be loud, but because they are out of control, they have lost their power. Perhaps, you see someone you love choosing a path that is dangerous or detrimental for them, but they won't listen. You have a friend who won't stop gossiping and lying even when they see how much they have hurt others. A nephew keeps stealing and suffering the consequences, but he just won't listen. Your brother is cheating on his wife. Hard work and dedication seem unrecognized by your boss. Patience means you have the fortitude to wait or endure time and be slow to anger. You can't do that on your own. To have that kind of patience requires the flow of the Holy Spirit. It doesn't mean you are complacent, permissive, or sit down and take things without taking a stand. It means you do what you need to do and you speak the truth in love, allowing individuals to be responsible for themselves. You aren't responsible for their decisions (unless they are your minor children or dependents) nor can you make their decisions for them. You do your part by speaking the truth. Speaking the truth means you speak God's Word of truth not your idea of truth. Once the truth is spoken then let it go. If you don't let it go and exercise patience, you can easily get into a pattern of attempting to control others. You can also dive deep into disappointment and discouragement. Not exercising patience and not letting go may also make you angry, which can turn to bitterness. That is never God's way. His will is patience.

How can you have that kind of patience? Patience that strong and powerful comes from the knowledge that God is all-powerful, all-knowing, and in total control of everything. When you know and believe God is who He says He is, then you can trust Him as Deliverer and have hope that He not only knows what's going on but is working in the middle of it. Without patience, you will have frustration that will attempt to rob you of joy. Keeping joy will depend on how patient or long-suffering you are. Just a reminder for your sanity and those who try your patience, long-suffering should always be endured in love. You may have the power to avenge yourself, but the attribute of long-suffering refrains you. When emotions rage and you want to act or react in passion, long-suffering helps you stay the course and repress the passionate emotional reaction. Long-suffering keeps you steadfast, not shifting to the right or the left but to keep moving forward no matter what is going on around you, how people are acting and reacting, or what your emotions want to do. Long-suffering shows well why the Fruits of the Spirit work as one. Patience, love, joy, self-control, peace, kindness all work together to minister to others.

"Strengthened with all might, according to His glorious power, to all patience and longsuffering with joy," Colossians 1:11.

Kindness

Kindness is the Greek word *chrestotes* used in Galatians 5 which means moral goodness or moral excellence, integrity, kindness, goodness, and gentleness. Moral goodness or moral excellence is **DOING WHAT IS RIGHT** and avoiding what is wrong. Things that are right line up with the will of God. This includes your attitude, values, goals, and priorities in all areas of your life. This fruit is about the kindness of your heart and your actions. Salvation comes to you through the kindness of the Lord. He restores you when you are weary, gathers you under His wings when you need protection. When you need the safety and comfort of your Creator, He gathers you in His arms and carries you close to His heart like He does the lambs in Isaiah 40:11.

"He shall feed his flock like a shepherd: he shall gather the lambs with his arm, and carry them in his bosom, and shall gently lead those that are with young." KJV

People can be rude and obnoxious. They can be selfish and abrasive. Some people think nothing about saying mean and hurtful things. Sometimes you can avoid them. Other times they are all up in your business. That's when you need kindness the most. Kindness has broken some of the stoutest, coldest hearts. Sometimes being kind to others requires a sacrifice for you. Kindness often requires selflessness because you put your own needs away while tending to the needs of another. It might be asking the lady in the checkout line if she needs help loading groceries in her car. Kindness says a kind word to someone who isn't kind to you. It chooses the right thing when others around you are choosing the wrong thing. It might not seem like this is kindness, but it is. If someone is making wrong choices, I guarantee someone will get hurt either physically or emotionally. To choose kindness is choosing to protect someone from the pain of a wrong choice. Believers should have a gentle spirit towards all people. That doesn't mean you let people walk all over you. It means you stand for righteousness with the compassion of Christ. Kindness is considering others in your actions and decisions. Kindness is allowing your words and actions to flow in the grace of the Lord.

"By pureness, by knowledge, by longsuffering, by kindness, by the Holy Ghost, by love unfeigned, by the word of truth, by the power of God, by the armour of righteousness on the right hand and on the left," 2 Corinthians 6:6-7 KJV.

Goodness

Goodness is a heart issue. The Greek word that translates as goodness in this passage is *agathosune*. The meaning of *agathosune* is virtue or beneficence. This is pure selflessness. Goodness is holiness in action. Righteousness motivates goodness. When you show goodness, you exhibit a desire to be a blessing to others for the benefit of that person and not just for the sake of doing something good. You sincerely want to show goodness to help or act selflessly. You may give to the poor, visit someone who is sick or lonely, volunteer, or even provide for your children. Lots of people do those things, but the difference is that goodness does these acts because of a heartfelt desire to make the other person's life better, and not just so you can feel better.

Goodness doesn't have to be mushy-gushy or goody-two-shoes, which in grade school lingo means someone who is always being good and probably for show or fear of parents or teachers. When you are 'good' out of your strength, it is to benefit you only. Because the fruit of goodness is a completely selfless act, it is not possible to operate in the fruit of goodness without the flow of the Holy Spirit. Goodness is a calm strength standing for righteousness on behalf of others. Confronting sin because you sincerely want to bring salvation to a lost soul is goodness. It isn't a quality such as 'she is a good girl' or a sense of value such as 'he has good taste.' Goodness is a virtuous characteristic that seeks only the best for others. Goodness is a level of moral excellence and character that is impossible to achieve without the Holy Spirit. The spiritual fruit of goodness will consist of holiness, grace, mercy, love, and righteousness. Goodness exhibits beauty and grace with the sole purpose of giving to others.

"For the fruit of the Spirit is in all goodness and righteousness and truth," Ephesians 5:9 KJV

FAITHFULNESS

Faithfulness is a key element in the lives of Christians. The Greek word used for faithfulness is *pistis*. The meaning is persuasion, specifically divine persuasion or guarantee. Faith is the conviction that God exists and is who He says He is. It is the tool by which you can receive the gift of salvation and fully commit your heart to Christ. Having strong faith builds confidence and assurance in whom and what you believe as a follower of Christ. Faithfulness is a strong allegiance to God's Word, His existence, and that He is who He says He is. For examples of men and women of faith, read Hebrews 11. Look up each of their trials and challenges and how God worked in their lives. Faith is a fruit that exhibits itself when life is most challenging.

Faithfulness is an unmovable trust that Jesus is salvation, the Messiah. It is a solid belief and trust that God is sovereign. He is the Creator, the Provider, the One who cares for you, and the One who loves you. It is the absolute conviction in Truth. Life happens and circumstances can be challenging, uncomfortable, painful, discouraging, disappointing, and depressing. Faithfulness is trusting God, despite whatever situations look like around you. On your own, you can't have that depth of faithfulness. It takes the Holy Spirit to grow faithfulness that can endure trials, tribulations, and the challenges of life. It took faithfulness for Daniel to trust God to protect him when he was thrown into a den of hungry lions. Faithfulness strengthened Noah to build an ark when he had never seen rain, and most everyone else believed water only came from the ground.

Faithfulness has a great deal of power. Faith brings the promises of God to reality. The sick are healed, blind eyes see, the lame walk, the deaf hear, miracles happen, debt dissolves, marriages change, children receive salvation, battles are won without fighting and so much more. Faith is a kingdom currency. Have you ever been to a bazaar? Pop-up lean-to's, filled with goods to barter, line the streets. There are flowers, lots of different food, clothing, hats, and so much more. You come to the bazaar of heaven with your basket of faith and go home with healing, deliverance, mercy, miracles, grace, and a multitude of promises from God. You hoped you might one day get these items. Faith makes it possible. You show your faith by being faithful. That means when you don't have enough to pay your bills, you trust God is Jehovah Jireh, the Lord my Provider. When the doctor says those horrible words, "it's cancer." You trust the Lord is Jehovah Rapha, the Lord my Healer. When the world is spinning out of control, you remain steadfast in faithfulness declaring He is Jehovah Shalom, the Lord my Peace. When you make a mistake and sin, faithfulness remembers He is Jehovah Tsidkenu, the Lord my Righteousness.

"Now faith is the substance of things hoped for, the evidence of things not seen," Hebrews 11:1 KJV.

"But without faith it is impossible to please Him, for he who comes to God must believe that He is, and that He is a rewarder of those who diligently seek Him," Hebrews 11:6.

Gentleness

Gentleness is not so much an action as it is a condition of the heart or an attitude. Gentleness is *prautes*, which is also translated as meekness. This fruit is probably the most misunderstood because many view gentleness backward. In American culture, meekness carries the connotation of weakness or cowardliness. That is not the true meaning of meekness. Gentleness or meekness is not about weakness but is about strength and power. Meekness is best described as perfect strength under control. Meekness has a lot more power than most want to give credit. I know it does, or the enemy wouldn't twist its meaning so drastically. The devil does not want you to have this fruit. It was the meekness and gentleness of Jesus that bought you back from the devil's power and gave you forgiveness as a child of God.

Meekness is an attitude of humility towards God and the understanding that He is ultimately in control. Jesus exemplified meekness while hanging on the cross. Though He had all power and could have come down off the cross at any moment, He didn't. He could have summoned leagues of angels. Yet, He submitted to the will of God and endured the cross for your sins. Your sins, not His for He had no sin. He carried your sin to the cross in meekness, submitting to the will of Father God.

Gentleness is enduring situations you know you have the power to retaliate and responding with patience, completely free of resentment. That is amazing strength. Gentleness/meekness is humbling yourself to the will of God. Gentleness is the opposite of anger and a desire for revenge. It doesn't mean you become a doormat. Gentleness means you are not easily offended and you forgive quickly. It isn't about being soft, but about acting in a loving, clear, encouraging manner, knowing the strength and power of God that lives within you.

I used to raise horses. A horse is about half a ton of sheer muscle. Those amazing, majestic powerhouses could have thrown and trampled me at any moment. They were much more powerful than me. You could feel their power ripple through their muscles when they moved. Yet, they submitted to my will. They did what I asked them to do with no attempts at revenge if they didn't like something we had to do. That is how you are to be toward others and the Lord. The weak let go of self-control and causing harm to those weaker than they are. The strong maintain self-control, submit to God, and flow in the Spirit of God in meekness/gentleness. If you have had the understanding that gentleness or meekness is a spineless way to act, ask the Lord to adjust your understanding and renew your mind, helping you to see the power in meekness.

"Brothers, if a man be overtaken in a fault, you which are spiritual, restore such an one in the spirit of meekness; considering yourself, lest you also be tempted," Galatians 6:1 AKJV.

"Let this mind be in you which was also in Christ Jesus, who, being in the form of God, did not consider it robbery to be equal with God, but made

Himself of no reputation, taking the form of a bondservant, and coming in the likeness of men. And being found in appearance as a man, He humbled Himself and became obedient to the point of death, even the death of the cross," Philippians 2:5-8.

TEMPERANCE

Temperance is from the Greek word *egkrateia*. It is sometimes interpreted as self-control. You know you cannot save yourself, but need the Holy Spirit to lead you to and minister salvation to you. Likewise, you cannot change your character through any self-help books, New Year's resolutions, or anything else. You need the Holy Spirit to grow and develop the character traits the Bible calls the Fruit of the Spirit. Temperance is the attribute of the Fruit of the Spirit by which the Holy Spirit empowers you to exercise control over your actions, thoughts, and emotions. It is the virtue of mastering your desires and passions, especially when it pertains to sensual desires. Every area of your life will exhibit temperance/self-control, from moderation in your eating habits to the ability to say 'no' to your baser desires. You can control your thoughts, which allow you to control your words, and ultimately control your actions. There are temptations all around. Temptations can be anything from eating too many cookies to much more damaging sexual affairs. They include thoughts that draw you to pornography, horoscopes, gossip columns, and anything ungodly. Temptations assault you as often as possible to draw you away from God. Temperance is the power to keep things in check. Self-control is the power to stay free. It keeps you free from guilt, shame, and remorse. Temperance keeps you from acting the fool and entertaining things or people that can enslave you. When people see you operating with self-control, it is a sign and a witness that the Lord is working in you and draws others to Him. Romans 6:6 says that *"knowing this, that our old man was crucified with Him, that the body of sin might be done away with, that we should no longer be slaves of sin."* The enemy wants to keep you a slave to sin. That's one reason he sends so many temptations your way. With the Holy Spirit flowing through you, temptations become like mosquitoes you swat and brush aside because you have given up slavery to sin and now walk in freedom. Temperance gives you the liberty to flow freely in all of your Spiritual Gifts and the Fruit of the Spirit. Without self-control, sin will wreak havoc in your life. With self-control, you open the door for the Gifts and Fruit of the Spirit to minister freely to others, giving God glory and drawing others to Him.

"For this very reason, make every effort to add to your faith goodness; and to goodness, knowledge; and to knowledge, self-control; and to self- control, perseverance; and to perseverance, godliness; and to godliness, mutual affection; and to mutual affection, love," 2 Peter 1:5-7.

Hindrances

The Fruit of the Spirit will not only change your life but change the lives of others. Remember, we talked about the trees in the forest in the Wizard of Oz. They had wonderful, nutritious fruit on them but refused to share. I hope you don't want to be like those nasty old trees. Trees don't grow fruit for themselves. They grow fruit to share and give to others. The Fruit of the Spirit developing you're your life is for you to share with others. There are, however, things that can hinder the development and use of the Fruit of the Spirit. The Lord has given you free will. Your will has the power to stop the development of these godly characteristics. Some things that can hinder the development and purposefulness of the Fruit of the Spirit are fear, high-mindedness, ignorance, unholy comparisons, neglect, quenching, worry, sin, and complacency. Let's take a brief look at each one. Just a note that these hindrances also block you from using your spiritual gifts so you may see reference to both the Fruit of the Spirit and/or spiritual gifts.

FEAR

Fear is an immobilizer. It is like a boa constrictor tight around the neck of life. Fear makes you afraid to move because you don't want to offend someone or you don't want their insults. It makes you afraid to love and be vulnerable. It deceives you so you have trouble figuring out what is truth. Fear overshadows trust and peace. It destroys confidence and blinds you so you miss opportunities. You have not been given a spirit of fear by God. He gave you the power of love.

"Therefore I remind you to stir up the gift of God which is in you through the laying on of my hands. For God has not given us a spirit of fear, but of power and of love and of a sound mind," 2 Timothy 1:6-7.

High-mindedness

Guess what? It's not about you. I know you want to think it's all about you. I know you want it to be all about you, but no. It's not about you at all. It's all about Jesus. Being high-minded is sometimes called egocentrism. Some might call it narcissism. That's okay for babies, but not so much for adults. Grown-ups with that mentality are haughty, manipulative, and full of pride. A high-minded person will tell you they are a good person with a good heart and yet make decisions that only promote themselves. High-mindedness tries to mask sin and twist it to make the sin seem like that of another person. High-mindedness is pretty dangerous because it usually leads others away from God, so is the opposite of the Fruit of the Spirit. The Bible tells you to not be high-minded and not to hang out with those who act high-minded. Always give glory to God and thank Him, remaining humble, and you will avoid high-mindedness.

"But know this, that in the last days perilous times will come: For men will be lovers of themselves, lovers of money, boasters, proud, blasphemers, dis-

obedient to parents, unthankful, unholy, unloving, unforgiving, slanderers, without self-control, brutal, despisers of good, traitors, headstrong, haughty, lovers of pleasure rather than lovers of God, having a form of godliness but denying its power. And from such people turn away!" 2 Timothy 3:1-5.

Ignorance

Ignorance is not stupidity. Ignorance is lack of knowledge. It means you can't do what you should do because you don't have the understanding or knowledge. There is a simple way to remedy this problem. Read the Word. The Bible is full of wisdom and understanding. There is information you need to know about all kinds of life situations throughout scripture, including your gifts and Spiritual Fruit. If you are ignorant of who you are in Christ and how to allow the Spirit of God to flow through you, just read the Bible and you will have the knowledge and understanding you need and the wisdom to use your gifts and fruit to honor God.

"Now concerning spiritual gifts, brethren, I do not want you to be ignorant," 1 Corinthians 12:1.

Comparisons

People are wired to put things into categories to better understand the world. You don't put your forks in the cabinet, your spoons in the bathroom, and the knives in the closet in the hall. No, all your tableware goes in the drawer in the kitchen together. Spoons are piled on spoons, forks are stacked on forks, and the knives go in that nice long part of the basket, all neat and tidy. It's what we do. Humans compare things to better sort them out for ease of use and understanding. It helps you remember things and keeps things in order. The problem with that is applying comparisons to people. Everyone can grow the Fruit of the Spirit. We all fit together like a finely woven tapestry, making something beautiful. However, if you compare your fruit to someone else, you risk the deceitful idea that their fruit is greater than yours. You might be a spoon in the drawer of life thinking the fork is so incredibly beautiful and wonderful with all its prongs and you are just a fat, round spoon. What good is a fork, though, if you want to eat soup? Your fruit and gifts are fine-tuned to fulfill the specific purpose that you were brought to this planet. No one else can fulfill it like you, and nobody is better than you. The Fruit is important and can only be used to its fullest potential at the right time and the right place by you through your specific purpose and destiny using your gifts and fruit.

"For in fact the body is not one member but many. If the foot should say, "Because I am not a hand, I am not of the body," is it therefore not of the body? And if the ear should say, "Because I am not an eye, I am not of the body," is it therefore not of the body? If the whole body were an eye, where would be the hearing? If the whole were hearing, where would be the smelling? But now God has set the members, each one of them, in the body just as He pleased," 1 Corinthians 12:14-18.

Neglect

We recently put our house on the market. As I was preparing it for showing, I found many problems. There was a spot on the ceiling where the roof had leaked. The rubber thing on the commode deteriorated and leaked water. Spiders had taken over the tub in the spare bathroom that we rarely used. There was a crack in the sidewalk and one of the ceiling fans had stopped working. There were marks on the kitchen wall that needed scrubbed or maybe we just needed to paint. When did all of this fall apart? We take care of our house. When the roof leaked, we fixed it. We dust and vacuum and don't leave messes lying around. We had just neglected the little things that needed repaired and simple upkeep. The same is true with the Fruit of the Spirit. If you neglect the fruit, there will be no development. The fruit will wither. You must water it. You can develop your fruit by feeding and watering it with scriptures. Then you will have ample fruit to give to others. Remember, the Fruit of the Spirit comes through the gift of the Holy Spirit to give to others to lead them to Christ. The more you give, the more you grow. You should not neglect the gift of the Holy Spirit. Holy Spirit is much too important and vital to your spiritual life to neglect.

"Do not neglect the gift that is in you, which was given to you by prophecy with the laying on of the hands of the eldership," 1 Timothy 4:14.

CRITICISM

Criticism comes from judgment. You judge others' faults and hand out disapproval. Criticism brings condemnation or blame which is the opposite of encouragement. Criticism is about fault-finding and quenches the Spirit through a critical attitude. Instead of bearing fruit, you become barren, not producing anything of worth. There is criticism done in love. Jesus spoke His disapproval of the actions of the Pharisees, but He did it in love and based it on truth. He wasn't fault-finding. He was speaking for righteousness. Big difference. Fault-finding is your opinion of someone else and is not based on the truth of God's word. If you know a Christian who is doing wrong, God is telling them about it. That doesn't mean they are listening or obeying, but I guarantee the Lord is showing them their wrongfulness. It isn't for you to keep count of their wrongdoings, but to love them back to Jesus. Those who are not Christian will always do wrong things and make unwise decisions, so you can expect that from them. Think about it. Was it someone berating you on how wrong you were about something that brought you to Jesus, or was it the Lord showing you and guiding you through love that guided you? I seriously doubt if any lasting attitude or heart changes came through any criticism. Criticism can be painful. Criticism makes you fruitless like King David's wife, Michal. She was highly and publically critical of her husband the king. She remained barren her whole life. No children. No fruit. Criticism quenches the work of the Spirit and fruit is most definitely a work of the Spirit.

"Do not quench the Spirit. Do not despise prophecies. Test all things; hold fast what is good. Abstain from every form of evil." 1 Thessalonians 5:19-22.

"Who are you to judge another's servant? To his own master he stands or falls. Indeed, he will be made to stand, for God is able to make him stand," Romans 14:4.

Worry

Worry is the opposite of faith, believing, and trusting. Worry happens when you don't trust. You might have heard the Word of God, and you know what it says. You can repeat it to others, but just don't quite know when it will apply to your life. The Word says God will supply all your needs according to His riches and glory, and yet you can't pay the car payment. Scripture says by His stripes you were healed and yet you are headed to another chemo appointment. The Word tells husbands to love their wives and wives to respect their husbands, and yet here you are yelling at each other in front of a judge. The Word says children are a blessing, yet you just got a call that your son was arrested for drug possession. You turn on the news and hear about fires, hurricanes, pandemics, racial injustices, killings, corruption, tsunamis, tornados, explosions, terrorists, wars, and on, and on. So many catastrophes and disappointments, and so you worry. That isn't what God has called you to do, though. He instructs you not to worry and to keep believing, keep trusting, and keep walking in faith. Worry will snatch the power of the Word right out of your heart and make your life unfruitful. Let worry go, and trust.

"Therefore I say to you, do not worry about your life," Matthew 6:25.

"Now he who received seed among the thorns is he who hears the word, and the cares of this world and the deceitfulness of riches choke the word, and he becomes unfruitful," Matthew 13:22.

Sin

There is sin everywhere and sin is contrary to the Spirit no matter how you look at it. If you are in sin, there will be no fruit except rotten fruit. In that case, you better pray for crop failure. It isn't just committing a sin that hinders the growth of fruit. It is your attitude toward sin. If you tolerate sin, treat it lightly, or act indifferently toward sin in yourself or others, then it can seriously damage your or someone else's life. Sin can trap fast and kill easily. Watch who you hang out with. Make sure that when God shows you your sin that you quickly repent and change your ways. When God shows you darkness in those you call friends, consider not spending time with them any longer. Fruit can't grow in the dark.

"And have no fellowship with the unfruitful works of darkness, but rather expose them," Ephesians 5:11.

COMPLACENCY

Complacency is about feeling all warm and fuzzy when danger is lurking at your door. It's about feeling self-satisfied and smug while completely unaware that danger is skulking around waiting for an opportunity. Though there is rest and contentment in God, there should never be complacency. Complacency is a form of self-righteousness. Your righteousness comes from Jesus and never from anything you do, say, or think. When you have a case of the warm fuzzies, you better think again. Complacency will hinder growth and productivity in the Spirit. You become lax and lazy instead of doing good works for others. Your righteousness does not come from your good works, but good works come from your righteousness. It's fine to rest and recharge. It's not fine to lead a life where you are oblivious to all that is around you and the dangers that seek to destroy you and your family, never reaching out to help others. Stay on guard while resting in the arms of Jesus and continue being fruitful.

"And let our people also learn to maintain good works, to meet urgent needs, that they may not be unfruitful," Titus 3:14.

Mountain vs. Valley

Before we finish, let's talk about where fruit grows. If you have been in Christianity for a minute or two, you have probably heard someone talk about a mountain top experience or how someone didn't enjoy walking through the valley. I get that because it's on the mountaintop where you meet God in a more face-to-face experience. It's a place of intimacy and revelation like you just can't get in the valley. Abraham met God on a mountain and received an understanding of the future of his descendants. Moses met God on the mountain and received the plan for Israel from the Law to the Promised Land. Jesus went up to the mountain to talk to the Father. God meets you on the mountaintop and you can see far into the future for specific situations and circumstances. The mountain experience is a place of intense worship and praise where you learn to bow low in this high and lofty place.

People compare their valley experiences as those times when adversity, trials, tribulation, discouragement, and many problems seem to come from a myriad of directions. Wars are fought in the valleys. Most people don't like being down in the valley. However, I challenge you to find the power in the valley experiences. Do you see fruit trees growing on top of mountains? Nope. Fruit grows in the valley. It's the adversity, trials, and tribulations that develop strong bearers of fruit. Trials build character.

I love vegetables right out of the garden, so I always try to grow a few things in the limited space I have. Tomatoes are one of my favorites from the garden, so tomatoes are the first plants I put in the garden. If I put them out early, I often put a milk jug over them while they are small to protect them from the elements and allow them to grow. Having them covered for a while is fine. Once I left the covering on too long. They grew very large, all cramped inside the jugs. When I took the jugs off, the first hard rain with a little wind broke the stems. Being all covered up had protected them too long from the elements, and they did not build resistance from adverse weather. When the first storm came, they snapped like dry twigs. They recovered, but it was a slow recovery. You live in a fallen world, so exposure to the adversities of life is inevitable. That's ok though because in the winds of adversity your faith grows and you gain strength and character. This makes you a productive person that cares for people through the love of God. So I have learned to embrace my valley experiences. I come out on the other side as a better, stronger person. I have a better understanding and compassion for others in similar situations.

Good soil that grows fruit trees is in the valley. The sun shines brightly in the valley. On the mountaintop are a lot of rocks and little sun. Love, joy, peace, patience, kindness, goodness, faithfulness, gentleness, and self-control thrive in the valley's richness. Does that mean fruit isn't on the mountaintop? Of course not. After all, the mountaintop is in the presence of God and He is Love, Joy, Peace, Patience, Kindness, Goodness, Faithfulness, Gentleness, and Temperance. It is in His presence;

you learn to be humble. So, when you are on the mountaintop, learn to bow low. When you are in the valley, stand tall as a tree of righteousness, bearing good fruit to give to all that pass by.

"He shall be like a tree planted by the rivers of water, that brings forth its fruit in its season, whose leaf also shall not wither; and whatever he does shall prosper," Psalm 1:3.

Stepping Stones

1. Love—The presence of the Holy Spirit showing unconditional, selfless love to others.

2. Joy—The presence of the Holy Spirit showing inexpressible and glorious rejoicing.

3. Peace—To rest easy in the knowledge and presence of the Holy Spirit.

4. Long-suffering—Enduring, steadfast perseverance in the Holy Spirit.

5. Kindness—By the power of the Holy Spirit, doing what is right and avoiding what is wrong.

6. Goodness—The holiness of God in action by the power of the Holy Spirit in you.

7. Faithfulness—Being fully committed in your heart to the Lord and fully persuaded His Word is true.

8. Gentleness—Submission to the Lord, which keeps your strength under control.

9. Temperance—Acquiring and maintaining self-control through the Holy Spirit.

10. The Fruit of the Spirit empowers you to show the character of God to others.

I Am Fruitful

WALKING IN THE FRUIT OF THE SPIRIT

1. Name the nine Fruit of the Spirit in Ephesians 5:22 and give a brief description of each.

2. Do you find it empowering to know that God's gift of the Holy Spirit is like a seed planted in you and growing fruit? Why or why not?

3. What fruit do you most recognize in yourself? Which fruit do you have the most trouble with?

4. What is the significance of 'Fruit' being singular rather than plural? Is it possible to show evidence of one fruit, but have the absence of other fruit?

5. How can you be more open to sharing the Fruit of the Spirit in the sphere of your influence?

Glossary

SIMPLE GLOSSARY OF A FEW WORDS FROM THE CHRISTIAN FAITH

Adultery - The act of being sexually unfaithful to one's spouse

Agape - Affection, goodwill, love, brotherly love, a love feast

Angel - Messenger of God

Apostasy - Turning away from the religion, faith, or principles that one used to believe

Apostle - One sent forth, one chosen and sent with a special commission as a fully authorized representative of the sender.

Atonement - To cover, blot out, forgive; restore harmony between two individuals.

Attribute – An inherent characteristic

Backslide - To go back to ungodly ways of believing or acting.

Blasphemy - Words or actions showing a lack of respect for God or anything sacred.

Bless - To make or call holy, to ask God's favor, to praise; to make happy.

Blessing - A prayer asking God's favor for something, something that brings joy or comfort.

Born-again – To be begotten or birthed from God, the beginning, to start anew

Carnal - Of the flesh or body, not of the spirit, worldly; seat of one's desires opposed to the spirit of Christ

Cherubim - Guardian angels, angels that guard or protect places

Commitment - A promise, a pledge

Conditional - Placing restrictions, conditions, or provisions to receive

Conversion - Turn, return, turn back; change

Convert - To change from one form or use to another, to change from one belief or religion to another.

Courtship - The act or process of seeking the affection of one with the intent of seeking to win a pledge of marriage

Covenant - A pledge, alliance, agreement

Cult - A body of believers whose doctrine denies the deity of Christ.

Deliverance - A freeing or being freed, rescue; the act of change or transformation.

Demon - Evil spirit

Devil - Principal title for satan, the archenemy of God and man

Dispensation - A period of time, sometimes called ages

Dominion - To rule over, have power over, overcome, exercise lordship over

Eros - Erotic, physical love

Eternal - Existing always, forever, without time

Evangelist - Proclaims the gospel of Jesus Christ

Faith - Believing, trusting, depending, and relying on God

Fellowship - Sharing, communion, partnership, intimacy

Forgiveness - To pardon, release from bondage

Fornication - To act like a harlot, to be unfaithful to God, illicit sexual intercourse

Glorification - Salvation of the body, transforming mortal bodies to eternal bodies

Grace - Unmerited favor of God, help given in the time of need from a loving God

Holy - Set apart, sacred

Intercession - To meet or encounter, to strike upon, to pray for another

Justification - Salvation of the spirit, just as if I never sinned

Marriage - A divine institution designed by God as an intimate union, which is physical, emotional, intellectual, social, and most importantly, spiritual

New Testament - Text of the new covenant

Offering - Everything you give beyond your tithe

Old Testament - Text of the old covenant

Omnipotent - All-encompassing power of God

Omnipresent - Unlimited nature of God, ability to be everywhere at all times

Omniscient - God's power to know all things

Pastor - Shepherds of the body of believers

Philia - Conditional love, based on feelings, friendships

Praise - Thanksgiving, to say good things about, words that show approval.

Prayer - Communication with God

Prophet - One who is a spokesperson for God, one who has seen the message of God and declares that message

Propitiation - To satisfy the anger of God, to gain favor; appease

Rapture - To be carried away, or the catching away of

Reconciliation - Restore harmony or fellowship between individuals, to make friendly again

Redemption - To buy back, to purchase, recover, to Rescue from sin

Regeneration - To give new life or force to, renew, to be restored, to make better, improve or reform, to grow back anew

Repent - To give new life or force, to renew, to be restored, to make better, improve or reform, to grow back a new.

Resurrection - A return to life subsequent to death

Revelation - The act of revealing or making known

Righteousness - Right standing with God, integrity, virtue, purity of life, correctness of thinking

Sacrifice - The act of offering something, giving one thing for the sake of another; a loss of profit

Salvation - Deliverance from any kind of evil whether material or spiritual, being saved from danger or evil; to rescue.

Sanctification - Salvation of the soul. Separation from the seduction of sin

Satan - The chief of fallen spirits, opponent; adversary

Sealing - Something that guarantees, a sign or token, to make with a seal to make it official or genuine

Sin - All unrighteousness, missing the mark, wrong or fault; violation of the law

Spirit - A being that is not of this world, has no flesh or bones

Steward - A guardian or overseer of someone else's property, manager

Supernatural - Departing from what is usual, normal, or natural to give the appearance of transcending the laws of nature

Talent - A natural skill that is unusual.

Tithe - Ten percent of all your increase

Tribulation - Distress, trouble, a pressing together, pressure, affliction

Trinity - Three in one: Father, Son, Holy Spirit

Unconditional - No restrictions, conditions, boundaries, demands, or specific provisions

Will – Choice, inclination, desire, pleasure, command, what one wishes or determines shall be done

About the Author

Pamela is a teacher, mentor, and author of the inspirational book *Destiny Arise* and children's books including *Time in a Tuna*. Pam earned her bachelor's degree at the University of Illinois Springfield, her master's degree in Organizational Leadership at Lincoln Christian University, and her doctorate in Leadership at Christian Leadership University. She serves as a mentor for the Spirit Life Circles sponsored by CLU.

She works from her home in the prairie land of central Illinois. Pam and her bodybuilding husband own a gym/fitness center that promotes living a balanced life. She taught sixth grade for almost twenty years. Pam also taught preschool through adult-age students in various venues. She served as director of Super Church, the children's ministry in the United Methodist Church in her hometown. Pam also served in the church nursery, as director of New Life Ministries Discipleship Program, Vacation Bible School Director, Kingdom Kids Children's Ministry Director, and Sunday School teacher. She has also been on missionary trips. Her favorite trip, so far, was the time she spent in Belize.

Pam enjoys kayaking, bicycling, and riding her motor scooter. When she isn't writing, she enjoys spending time with her four children and their families which includes five grandchildren who are the inspiration of her children's books.

Walking with Jesus Series

Becoming the Best Me I Can Be

Book 1 - There Must Be a Better Way
Walking in Salvation

Book 2 - Lord, I Need Help!
Walking with the Holy Spirit

Book 3 - I Thought I Was Changed
Walking in Transformation

Book 4 - I Am Supernatural
Walking in Spiritual Gifts

Book 5 - I Am Strong
Walking as a Warrior

Book 6 - I Am Fruitful
Walking in the Fruit of the Spirit

Book 7 - Love Letters from God
Walking in the Word

Book 8 - Time in the Garden
Walking in the Power of Prayer

Book 9 - I'm in Charge of What?
Walking in Stewardship

Book 10 - The End of – Well, Pretty Much Everything
Walking into Eternity

Who am I? What am I doing here? Where am I going? Everyone at some point in life asks these questions. You were wired to ask and engineered to pursue the answers. The road to discovering destiny is besieged by fiascoes, failures, and the agony of defeat. If your strength has been depleted and has caused you to give up, sit down, push pause, and snooze until another day, then this book is just for you! Amazing experiences are waiting for you. Get ready to be awakened from the posture of defeat, depression, and despair.

Destiny Arise is an easy-to-read book, providing tools to aid in living an amazing life. This book is designed as a trip adviser for your expedition. It will teach you how to evict the spirit of mediocrity and use your past to propel you into your future. You will learn how to shake off the common, arising to be an uncommon force taking your rightful place in the earth. You can change the world. I pray this book will ignite a passionate fire to pursue your destiny unapologetically. Destiny, awake from your slumber and arise.

www.ingramcontent.com/pod-product-compliance
Lightning Source LLC
Chambersburg PA
CBHW062202100526
44589CB00014B/1919